How to Be a Scientist

Prove It!
The Scientific Method in Action

Susan Glass

Heinemann Library
Chicago, Illinois

ʾary

ʾier Inc.

Chicago, Illinois

Customer Service 888–454–2279

Visit our website at www.heinemannlibrary.com

Photo research by Ruth Blair and Ginny Stroud-Lewis
Designed by Victoria Bevan and AMR Design Ltd
Printed in China by WKT Company Ltd

11 10 09 08
10 9 8 7 6 5 4 3 2

Library of Congress Cataloging-in-Publication Data
Glass, Susan.
 Prove it! : the scientific method in action / Susan Glass.
    p. cm. -- (How to be a scientist)
 The Scientific method -- Classroom experiments -- Taking it further -- Tying it together
 -- Careers using the scientific method -- Scientific method flowchart.
 Includes bibliographical references and index.
 ISBN-13: 978-1-4034-8359-1 (library binding (hard cover))
 ISBN-10: 1-4034-8359-0 (library binding (hard cover))
 ISBN-13: 978-1-4034-8363-8 (pbk.)
 ISBN-10: 1-4034-8363-9 (pbk.)
 1. Science--Methodology--Juvenile literature. 2. Science--Experiments--Juvenile literature.
 3. Science--Vocational guidance--Juvenile literature. I. Title. II. Series: Glass, Susan. How to
 be a scientist.
 Q175.2.G576 2007
  507.2--dc22
               2006010639

Acknowledgments
The author and publisher are grateful to the following for permission to reproduce copyright material: Alamy Images pp. 26 (Bob Pardue), 34 (Gari Wyn Williams), 7 (Leslie Garland Picture Library), 30 (Roger Bamber); Art Directors & Trip p. 38; Corbis pp. 8, 39; Corbis pp. 4 (Bettmann), 14 (Bruce Chambers/Orange County Register), 31 (Karl Ammann); Getty Images p. 5 (Photodisc); Harcourt Education pp. 9, 27 (Ginny Stroud-Lewis); 11, 12, 15, 16, 16, 20, 21, 22, 25, 25, 28, 32, 33 (Tudor Photography); Mary Evans Picture Library p. 37; Science Photo Library pp. 24 (B.W.HOFFMAN / AGSTOCK), 18 (CORDELIA MOLLOY), 10 (DAVID HAY JONES), 43 (JAMES KING-HOLMES / FTSS), 40 (JEREMY BISHOP), 6 (KENT WOOD), 42 (MICHAEL DONNE), 41 (NASA), 36 (PHILIPPE PLAILLY / EURELIOS), 19 (SUSUMU NISHINAGA), 23 (TOM MCHUGH).

Cover photograph of fluid dropping from a pipette into a test tube reproduced with permission of Alamy Image/Stockfolio

The publishers would like to thank Bronwen Howells for her assistance in the preparation of this book.

Every effort has been made to contact copyright holders of any material reproduced in this book. Any omissions will be rectified in subsequent printings if notice is given to the publisher.

Dedication
I would like to thank my husband, John, for all his help and encouragement. I want to dedicate this book to him, my parents, my children Joanna, John, Billy, and Tricia, and my granddaughter Madison.

Disclaimer
All the Internet addresses (URLs) given in this book were valid at the time of going to press. However, due to the dynamic nature of the Internet, some addresses may have changed, or sites may have changed or ceased to exist since publication. While the author and publishers regret any inconvenience this may cause readers, no responsibility for any such changes can be accepted by either the author or the publishers.

Contents

Some words are shown in bold, **like this**. You can find out what they mean by looking in the glossary.

Anthrax

In May 1881 in Melun, France, a crowd had come to see the scientist Louis Pasteur. He was about to prove that he could save animals from **anthrax**. This disease had killed half the cattle and sheep in France. Farmers were desperate to save their animals from it.

Pasteur had done **investigations** with anthrax **bacteria**. He discovered that injecting weakened anthrax bacteria into animals made them a little sick, but not sick enough to die. Later he gave them a stronger dose. This time, the animals' bodies could recognize the bacteria and defend themselves. The animals did not get sick. Pasteur had made a **vaccine** that protected the animals from this deadly disease.

Around 50 sheep were brought before the crowd. Half were injected with Pasteur's vaccine. Half were not. Weeks later all were given deadly doses of anthrax. Most of the unvaccinated sheep collapsed and died in two days. But every single vaccinated sheep lived!

Louis Pasteur's work saved many people and animals.

Scientists use the scientific method in their research.

Finding answers

Pasteur developed the anthrax vaccine using a process called the **scientific method**. Pasteur investigated **microbes**, living things so small they can only be seen with a microscope. He asked questions about microbes and conducted **experiments** to find the answers. These investigations led to more questions and answers.

By using the scientific method, Pasteur also developed a vaccine for rabies. Rabies is a killer disease that can pass from rabid animals to humans through a bite. He tested the rabies vaccine on dogs. It worked. He wanted to test it on people so badly that he considered injecting himself. Then a rabid dog bit a nine-year-old boy. The boy would die if the vaccine did not work. Pasteur gave him the shots and the boy lived!

DID YOU KNOW?

Louis Pasteur used the scientific method to prove that heat kills microbes in milk and other liquids. Pasteurization—heating food or drinks to kill microbes—is named for him. You probably drink pasteurized milk. Read the container and find out!

The scientific way

The word *science* comes from an old word, *scientia*, meaning "to know." Science is a way to study the world around us. It is an exciting search for what is true. The word *method* means "a way of doing something." The scientific method is the scientific way of finding things out.

See and ask

By using the scientific method, scientists investigate things in an orderly, exact way. They start by asking a question about an **observation**. It has to be a question with an answer you can prove. Pasteur's question was about how to stop microbes from making animals and people sick.

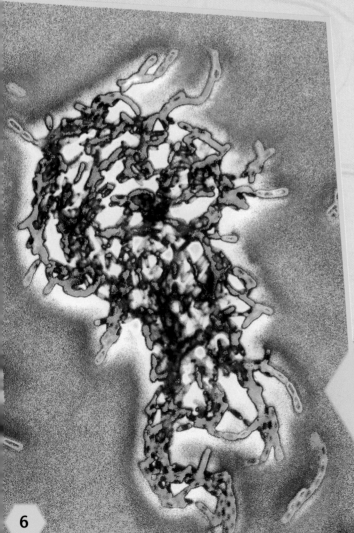

Test and tell

The next step in the scientific method is to come up with a **hypothesis**, or what might be an answer to a question. A hypothesis is a possible answer that can be tested. Scientists do research to see what has already been learned. Research tells them if someone else has already found the answer to their question.

These are anthrax bacteria. Louis Pasteur used a weakened version in his vaccine.

What can you observe about these rocks?

TRY IT!

How carefully do you observe? Take a handful of rocks. Write a description of each that tells its color, size, weight, shape, texture, and markings. See if others can identify each rock from your descriptions.

After creating a hypothesis, scientists plan and conduct an experiment. They take careful **measurements** and keep records of them. Scientists must give detailed descriptions of the things they do and observe in their experiments. That way others can understand and repeat their experiments. It is important for scientists to record the things they see by taking notes. Videos and photographs are also good ways to keep records. Records are important!

The **results** of an experiment prove a hypothesis to be right or wrong. After completing an experiment, scientists share what they find out with others.

These steps form the scientific method:

1. Observe and ask questions
2. Form a hypothesis
3. Plan an experiment
4. Conduct the experiment
5. Draw **conclusions** and communicate results

The Scientific Method

People first used the scientific method as we know it around 500 years ago, during a time called the **Renaissance**. The newly invented printing press printed many books very quickly. Books allowed people to learn about the world. They also allowed scientists to learn about the research other scientists had completed.

Soon knowledge spread. People such as Galileo Galilei tested things and wrote books about their discoveries. For example, Galileo was the first to prove that a heavy object did not fall faster than a light object when dropped. Galileo was probably the first person to use the experimental scientific method we use. You can follow it too.

In this painting the Renaissance scientist Vesalius is studying the human body.

Scientists do not always stick to the five steps of the scientific method (see page 7). They sometimes investigate in other ways. They might design and make things, gather information, or put things into groups. The ways scientists investigate things may vary, but it is important for them to know and understand how to use the scientific method.

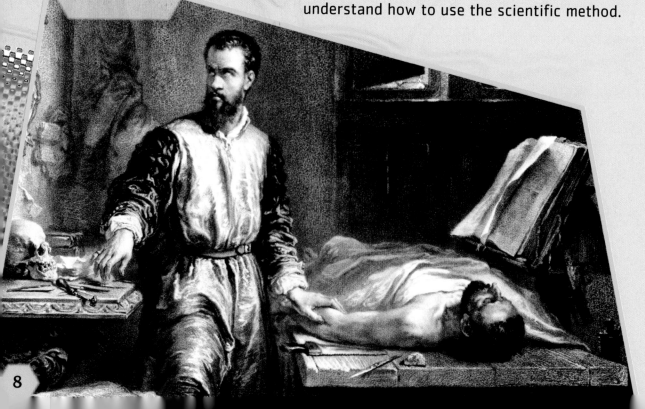

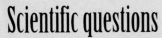
Before the Renaissance, one question people used to think about was, "How many angels can stand on the point of a pin?" That is not a question for which you could plan an experiment. It does not work as a science question because you cannot investigate it to prove the answer.

Scientific questions

Science begins with a question, but not just any question. It has to be one with an answer that you can prove. If it is a question like "How do I make a **model** volcano?" or "How do I make an electromagnet?" and all you do is follow directions to make it, then it is not really an experiment. It is just following directions.

Imagine that you want to plan an experiment with your dog. First you must come up with a question. "What is my dog thinking?" would be hard to prove, so that is not a good choice. But "Does my dog like Brand X dog food better than Brand Y?" is a question that you could answer with an experiment.

Scientific questions have answers that can be proved.

9

Observe, hypothesize, and plan

A hypothesis is what you think is the answer to a question. It is based on observations and research. Perhaps you saw your dog eat Brand X dog food and that observation made you think: "My dog likes Brand X food better than Brand Y." That could be your hypothesis.

Once you have a hypothesis, the next step in the scientific method is to design your experiment. Taking measurements is an important part of an experiment. Just looking at something is not always accurate. Instead you must weigh it or use measuring cups. Saying "he ate more Brand X food," would not be scientific. However, saying that "he ate one cup" or "he ate 100 grams" of Brand X food is scientific. Recording measurements is also an important part of an experiment.

Scientists conduct experiments to discover whether their hypotheses are true.

Use measurements. Change only one variable at a time. Here, the variable is the food brand.

A fair test

Variables are things that can be changed. They can affect how the experiment turns out. Your experiments should test only one variable (called the independent variable) at a time. In this case the brand of food is the independent variable. Changing just one variable is called a fair test. Everything else is kept the same.

Try to think of everything that could possibly make your dog eat more of one dog food than the other. Perhaps your dog is hungrier in the morning than in the evening. You should put both brands out at the same time. That way, you know your dog is not going to be more or less hungry if you put the bowls out at different times.

Keep all other variables the same except for the one thing you are testing—the brand. Use **identical** dishes so that your dog does not choose one dish over another. Make sure the food is equally fresh. If the food comes in different flavors, make sure they are the same for each brand. Do the test at the same time each day. Record your results carefully so others can replicate, or copy, your experiment.

Once is not enough

Using the scientific method involves completing many tests. If you only tested your dog's food choice at one meal it might not give you a true picture. Maybe that day he just happened to feel like eating Brand Y. Perhaps tomorrow he would go back to Brand X. Test your hypothesis over several days at the same time each day.

Repeat the test many times to ensure that you have an accurate result.

Scientists never test something just once. If they tested a new fertilizer on just one strawberry plant and it did not grow well, they could not be sure that it was the fertilizer's fault. Maybe it was just a weak plant or maybe someone pinched the stem too hard. Who knows? Instead, scientists test new fertilizers on a **sample** of strawberry plants. A sample is a limited group that is studied in order to learn about the whole group.

Conclusions and results

Results are what happened during an experiment. Results of the dog food test would tell you how much of each food your dog ate at each meal. You would write down the dates you did the experiment and the amounts of each dog food your dog ate. You would also write down any other observations you made. Did your dog eat all of one bowl before he started the other? Did he always eat the same brand first?

Any details to give others a good idea of how an experiment went are helpful. When sharing an experiment with others, you should show them your results. A bar **graph**, line graph, or circle graph are good ways to display your findings.

Every experiment has a conclusion. When you are done testing and you have looked over all your notes and compared the numbers, how did it turn out? Was your hypothesis correct according to your results? Was it proven wrong? Either way, you win. The point is to find out the answers, not to be right. If you are like Pasteur, your conclusion might lead you to the next investigation.

Record your results and observations. Other people should be able to understand your experiment results.

Results: Amount of dog food eaten (in grams)

	Brand X	Brand Y
Day 1	50	50
Day 2	75	50
Day 3	100	25
Day 4	100	50
Day 5	100	0
Day 6	100	75
Day 7	100	25

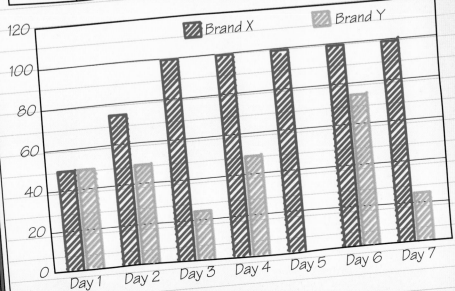

Classroom Experiments

Companies use the scientific method to test their products. **Consumer groups** test them too. That way they can advise people about which products are good to buy and which ones are not.

We have all seen commercials that say one brand of paper towel **absorbs** (soaks up) water better than other brands. One class decided to test paper towels for themselves by using the scientific method. They chose four brands of paper towels to test. We can call them Brands A, B, C, and D.

1 Observe and ask questions

The students came up with the question, "Which paper towel absorbs the most water?" This was a question that they could prove an answer to by experimenting. Before they came up with a hypothesis they learned what they could. They began with their own observations. They researched advertisements. They read the packaging. They noticed which towels seemed thicker.

They also did research by asking adults about the brands they used and which ones the adults thought absorbed best. Then they were ready to make a hypothesis.

You can test products. Do they live up to their claims?

How would you decide which towel absorbs more water?

② Form a hypothesis

Based on their research and observations, the class decided that Brand A would absorb the most water. They chose Brand A because it had the thickest sheets. The sheets felt thicker and a stack of twenty sheets was taller when measured. The commercials and packaging for Brand A also said that it absorbed the most.

③ Plan an experiment

The students had to decide how to do the experiment. They needed a way to measure the amount of water each paper towel soaked up. There were many possibilities. They could measure one cup of water, dip a paper towel into it, and then record how much water was taken out of the cup. Or they could pour one teaspoon of water at a time onto each towel and count how many teaspoons each one held.

4 Conduct the experiment

The students decided that the best way to complete the experiment was to wet each towel in a bowl of water. They would then squeeze the water out into a measuring jug and measure how much water came from each paper towel. They decided to test three paper towels from each brand.

The students realized they could get a more exact measurement of the water if they poured it from the measuring jug into a **graduated cylinder**. They wrote down the amount of water in milliliters that was squeezed from each paper towel. Then all they had to do was add up the three amounts for each brand to see which paper towel had absorbed the most.

Decide on the best way to get measurements.

Draw conclusions and communicate results

To show their results, the students used a bar graph of the totals for each brand. It clearly showed which had absorbed the most. The group decided to find the average amount absorbed by each brand by dividing each total by three. They also made a graph of the averages.

Brand C had absorbed the most water. The class decided that their hypothesis was proven false by their results. But they knew that the experiment was a success. They had learned something by using the scientific method. They showed others their notes and graphs of the results.

Every experiment can lead to others. Some members of the class thought that it would have been better if they had weighed the paper towels. Maybe the paper towels were not squeezed exactly the same way each time. Some of the group decided that they wanted to see which paper towel was strongest. They started planning an experiment to test that.

Display your results on graphs or charts.

Results (in milliliters):

	1st test	2nd test	3rd test
Brand A	19	17	18
Brand B	13	14	12
Brand C	22	23	21
Brand D	11	10	12

Growing mold

Product testing is just one way the scientific method affects people's lives. But the scientific method can be applied to lots of things we notice in the world around us. For example, one student opened a loaf of bread from the kitchen cupboard and discovered mold on it.

He began to wonder where mold comes from. He looked up the word *mold* in the encyclopedia and on the Internet. He found out that mold is a **fungus**. A fungus gets its food from living things or from something that came from a living thing. His bread was made from things that were once alive. Wheat flour, for example, comes from plants. His bread could be food for a fungus!

He wondered how the mold got on his bread. He read that fungi put out lots of microscopic cells called **spores**. People do not notice spores because they are too small to see. But they are just about everywhere.

When a spore lands on something it can use for food, it starts to grow. Molds can grow in a lot of places but they do best in warm, moist places. The student suggested to his class that they should try to grow some mold.

Mold can digest bread. This slice is covered in mold.

1 Observe and ask questions

The students discussed mold. They wanted to come up with a question they could answer by doing an experiment. Someone suggested that they should see if their classroom floor had as many mold spores as on the dirt outside. The class liked the idea. They asked, "Are there as many mold spores on the classroom floor as on the dirt outside?"

2 Form a hypothesis

Next the class needed a hypothesis based on their observations and research. They thought that since the floor was cleaned every day, the spores would get picked up. So they **predicted** the floor would have fewer spores. The class made the hypothesis, "The classroom floor has fewer mold spores than the dirt outside."

This is how bread mold looks when viewed under a powerful microscope.

③ Plan an experiment

The class had to design an experiment to test their hypothesis. Their teacher told them that many people are allergic to mold so they should grow it in see-through sandwich bags that could be sealed. The class thought the bags would also keep the bread from drying out. Mold needs moisture. Someone suggested they place a folded up, wet paper towel in each bag to make sure the bread stayed moist.

④ Conduct the experiment

The students took one loaf of bread and pressed ten slices gently into several different spots on the dirt outside. They then put the slices into separate sandwich bags with the wet paper towels inside. They took ten other slices and pressed those against several different spots on the classroom floor. These were also slipped into the bags along with wet paper towels. All the sandwich bags were sealed. They labeled each bag "Dirt" or "Floor."

Label the bags and keep them sealed. Each slice of bread needs the same controlled conditions.

FLOOR 2

DIRT 2

The students then placed all the bags in a cupboard. That way they were sure that no one was touching them and that they were the same temperature. Putting them all in the cupboard kept the conditions the same for all the slices.

After a few days, mold began to appear on each slice of bread. The group decided that they would compare the slices one week from the day they bagged them. After one week, all the slices had mold. The ones that had been pressed into the dirt had more mold than the ones pressed onto the floor. The students measured the amount of mold by placing **centimeter squares** on the sandwich bags where there was mold. They counted and recorded the squares for each slice. They also took photos of the slices.

⟨5⟩ Draw conclusions and communicate results

All ten slices pressed in the dirt had more mold. The students' hypothesis was proven correct. The results of the experiment were displayed in graphs and photos for others to see.

Photos are a good way to record your results. You could keep a photo-record of how the mold develops.

Controls and Blind Tests

Scientists follow the same basic process when they use the scientific method. They may also use additional tools to help them complete their experiments. Some tools—including **controls**, blind tests, models, and animals—are best used with certain types of experiments.

Experiments with a control

In some experiments it is a good idea to use a control. When using a control, you leave out the thing you are testing. Imagine you wanted to know if bleach really lifts grass stains from laundry. You would compare grass-stained clothes washed with bleach to grass-stained clothes that were washed without bleach. Those washed without bleach would be the control.

This experiment to see if fertilizer is effective will not work unless all the variables, including sunlight, are controlled.

Control groups

Scientists have learned many things by using control groups. For example, scientists wanted to know if people who live with those who smoke were more likely to get lung **cancer**. They did research to compare lung cancer rates of those who lived with a smoker to lung cancer rates of people who did not. The second group was the control group. They discovered that people who live with a smoker are at a higher risk of getting lung cancer. One study even found that smokers' dogs are more likely to get lung cancer!

A rattlesnake eating prey. Scientists can discover more about animals by using the scientific method.

DID YOU KNOW?

Rattlesnakes bite their prey and let them get away. Then they follow their poisoned victims before eating them. Scientists thought that the snakes followed the scent of their own venom, or poison. They conducted an experiment with a control. They dragged dead mice that had been bitten by a rattlesnake and the snake followed their trails. Then they dragged dead mice that had not been bitten. This was the control. The snake did not follow.

Sunlight's effect on plants

A group of students wanted to know if sunlight makes seedlings, the young plants that grow from seeds, grow taller.

1 Observe and ask questions

The students first found out what they could about seeds and seedlings. They looked in books and on the Internet. They asked adults. They learned that a seed needs water to sprout. They knew that plants need sunlight to make their own food.

2 Form a hypothesis

The students based their hypothesis on the information they had found. Their hypothesis was, "Seedlings will grow taller in a sunny place than in a dark one."

3 Plan an experiment

The students decided to test their hypothesis by conducting an experiment using seeds. They made sure the seeds were from the same packet. They decided to plant twelve seeds in identical containers, with identical potting soil. Each seed was planted at the depth the packet recommended.

Here the progress from seed to healthy seedling plant is shown.

4 Conduct the experiment

The students placed six seed containers
on a sunny counter. Six others sat in a dark
cupboard. This second group was the control.
In the control group the thing the students
are testing—sunlight—had been removed.

The students watered both groups of plants with the same
amount of water. The only difference was that one group
got sunlight. The other group was in the dark. When the
plants sprouted, they measured the height of the seedlings
every other day for two weeks.

5 Draw conclusions and communicate results

The students photographed the plants after two weeks
and graphed the measurements of the plants. To their
surprise, the whole group in the dark grew far taller than
the group in the sun! The results of their experiment
had proved their hypothesis wrong.

When they did more research, they learned that each seed
contains food for the baby plant. The seedling uses that
food to grow until it finds light. Then its leaves use the
sunlight to make food for the plant. The plants in the dark
grew very tall because they were seeking light. If they had
stayed in the dark long enough they would have died
when the food in the seed ran out.

> Everything in this
> experiment is the
> same, except for
> the light.

Blind tests

If an experiment has to do with people instead of plants, things get more complicated. People can be **subjective**. A person's mood, attitudes, or thoughts might influence what she or he sees or does. Plants are not subjective. They will always react the same way.

A person's expectations can affect the results of an experiment without anyone realizing it. For example, if a person believes that a pill will make them better, sometimes that belief can make it happen. To keep a person's opinions and feelings from having an effect on the outcome of an experiment, scientists perform blind tests. In a blind test, the person being experimented on does not know whether they are part of the control group.

In double-blind tests, neither the doctor nor the patient knows who will get the real medicine.

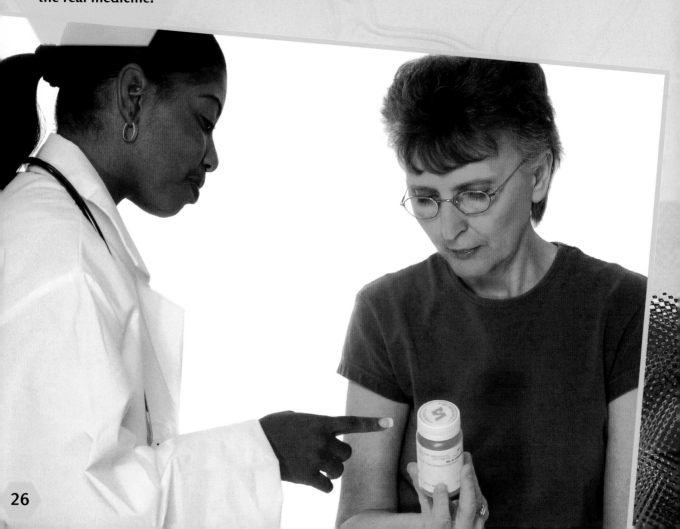

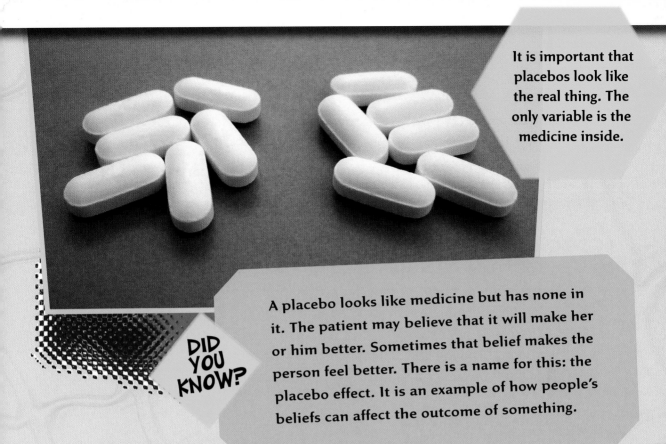

It is important that placebos look like the real thing. The only variable is the medicine inside.

DID YOU KNOW?

A placebo looks like medicine but has none in it. The patient may believe that it will make her or him better. Sometimes that belief makes the person feel better. There is a name for this: the placebo effect. It is an example of how people's beliefs can affect the outcome of something.

Placebos

Blind testing is often used in medical experiments. Doctors and patients agree to these tests. When a new medicine is tested researchers use a control. They have doctors give out pills containing medicine to some patients. They also give out pills with no medicine in them to other patients. The pills with no medicine are called **placebos**. Doctors and patients know this is going on. They understand they might get placebos.

Double-blind experiments

Patients do not know if they are getting a placebo or the real medicine. If they knew, then it could have an effect on the outcome. The people getting the placebos are the control group. In some cases even the doctors giving the pills do not know if they are giving out the real medicine or the placebos. Perhaps the doctor would act differently and affect the outcome. When neither the doctor nor the patient knows which group is the control, it is called a double-blind study.

Taste test

Many makers of foods and drinks do taste tests when they want to know if people like the taste of their product. During these tests they do not let tasters know which brand is which. That way, tasters' opinions will not affect the outcome. It is a blind test.

① Observe and ask questions

When it comes to food and drink, you could test all kinds of things such as juice, bottled water, or popcorn brands. One class decided to test two brands of orange juice. They looked at the claims made by the juice makers about the taste of the juices. They asked people which they preferred. They even called a supermarket to ask which brand sold more.

② Form a hypothesis

They based their hypothesis on the information that had been gathered. Their hypothesis was that Brand 1 would win the taste test.

③ Plan an experiment

The students thought of variables that could change how things turned out. They knew they must make certain that all testers did not know which brand they were drinking. Testers might pick the one they expected to like without realizing it. Even the students serving the juice should not know which was which. That way, they could not accidentally give testers clues.

This is a double-blind test. Neither the servers nor the tasters know the brands.

④ Conduct the experiment

Brand 1 was poured into cups labeled "Drink 1." Brand 2 was poured into cups labeled "Drink 2." All other variables had to be kept the same—the amount of juice, the temperature, the freshness, and the type of cups.

Several students tasted and recorded their preference. They took care not to let others know their choice because it might influence them. Then a student collected and added the results.

⑤ Draw conclusions and communicate results

Twelve students preferred Drink 1 and twelve students chose juice Drink 2. Four students liked them equally well. The group displayed their results on a chart. They shared their results with another class. The results did not support the hypothesis. The students learned that in taste tests done by product makers, thousands of tasters are used to get a clear picture of which brands they prefer.

Display your results in an easy-to-read way, such as this pie-chart.

Results:
Preferred juice 1: ‖‖‖‖ ‖‖‖‖ ‖‖
Preferred juice 2: ‖‖‖‖ ‖‖‖‖ ‖‖
Liked both equally: ‖‖‖

Both
4

Juice 1
12

Juice 2
12

Animals and Models

Animals can be very interesting to investigate. Some scientists do experiments with animals in zoos and labs. Other scientists study animals in the wild. They have learned about animal intelligence and behavior. Animal studies have helped people understand humans and nature better.

Keeping it safe

Animal behavior investigations are okay as long as you are certain to do no harm. Animals, even tiny **invertebrate** ones like insects, should not be made to suffer. You should remember that wild things, even bugs, should not be kept for long periods of time.

You should keep yourself safe too. Wash your hands after touching animals, and do not get bitten! Also remember that animals are complicated. There are many things that could affect their behavior. It might be harder to tell what caused an experiment's results if you are dealing with cats than if you are dealing with plants.

Scientists are careful with animal subjects and their environments.

30

Testing pets and wild animals

You could do investigations at home with your pets. Think of a question you could ask that you could answer with experiments. Which family member does your dog wag his tail most for? Does your lizard care what color his food is? Can your hamster find her way through a maze faster the second time around?

You could also study invertebrates. Snails, ants, worms, and other invertebrates are animals too. What kind of leaves do snails or ants prefer? Scientists say that ants follow the trail left by their scouts. What happens if you clean the trail? Can they still follow it? There are many possibilities for investigations with animals, just be careful not to harm the animal subjects you are testing.

Jane Goodall used photographs to record many of her observations of chimpanzee behavior.

DID YOU KNOW?

Jane Goodall studied wild chimpanzees in Africa. She sat and watched them for many years, taking lots of notes and photos, and building up her knowledge. She learned that they used tools. She also learned they can wage war on each other just as humans do. Goodall's work helped us understand both chimps and humans better.

Experimenting with wood lice

A group of students planned an investigation to learn more about wood lice.

1 **Observe and ask questions**

The students tried to answer the question, "Do wood lice prefer damp surroundings or dry ones?" They looked up *wood lice* in the encyclopedia and on the Internet.

2 **Form a hypothesis**

Based on their observations and research, the students' hypothesis was: "Wood lice prefer damp surroundings."

3 **Plan an experiment**

The students decided to trap several wood lice without harming them. To do so, they cut a potato in half lengthwise and scooped out the center. Next, they joined the halves together with toothpicks. They cut a small tunnel to the center. They left the trap in a garden overnight. The next day, it was full of wood lice.

This potato has been hollowed out and secured with toothpicks to make a damp, dark wood lice trap.

You can see a few wood lice on the damp side, and none on the dry side.

4 **Conduct the experiment**

The group placed a dry paper towel on one half and a damp paper towel on the other half of the bottom of a shoebox. They dropped twenty wood lice in the middle and covered the box with the lid. After two minutes, they lifted the lid and quickly counted the number of bugs on each side of the box. The test was repeated several times.

5 **Draw conclusions and communicate results**

On the first two tries, all twenty were on the damp side. On the third try, nineteen were on the damp side and one was on the dry side. On the fourth and fifth tries, eighteen were on the damp side, one on the dry side, and one in the middle. The class went to recess. When they returned and did the final test, half the wood lice were on the dry side and half on the damp.

The results of five out of six trials supported the hypothesis. The students graphed their results and displayed them. They turned the wood lice loose in the garden so they could go free.

It started to rain right after the last try. One student hypothesized that the air was so full of moisture that the animals were damp even on the dry side. Finding that out would take a different experiment.

Experiments using models

Sometimes scientists use models to answer questions. In science, models are small representations of something. If you wanted to know if fat helps a whale keep warm, it would be hard to test on a real whale. But you could wrap something small in fat and use a thermometer to see if it stayed warm. That would be using a model.

Storms, the inside of the Earth, and **galaxies** are just a few subjects that are too large or difficult to work with. Computers can be very useful when it comes to exploring these subjects. Scientists put information into computers to make models of different things.

Shadows change length as the sun changes position during the day.

You can be a model!

Do you ever wonder how tall a tree or building is? One ancient scientist reasoned that he could measure a building's shadow to find out how tall it was. Shadows are longest when the Sun appears low in the sky. They are shortest when the Sun is high. Of course, the Sun seems to move across the sky because our Earth is spinning.

The scientist figured out that if he found out what time of day the length of his shadow matched his height, he could measure the building's shadow at the same time. The length would be the same as the height of the building. He asked a question, then figured out a way to answer it by testing it out on a model—his own body and its shadow.

TRY IT!

Have someone measure your height. Then find a spot outside where you can mark a line with that same measurement on the ground. Make the line go in the direction your shadow is going. Stand at the end of it at different times of day. When your shadow is the same length as the line, measure the shadow of a building or tree. This measurement will equal its height.

When your shadow reaches your height measurement (59 inches in this case), measure the tree's shadow.

Sun

29 feet

59 inches (150 cm)

59 inches

29 feet (9 meters)

Tying It Together

Real scientists write papers or books about the results and details of their experiments. That way other scientists can copy their experiments and see if their results are similar. If other scientists cannot repeat their experiments and get the same kind of results, then nothing has been proven.

Sometimes scientists make mistakes. Having other scientists do the same experiment again helps correct those mistakes.

A mistaken claim

In 1989 two scientists made the claim that they had found a way of creating energy called **cold fusion**. The scientists were on the covers of magazines, on TV, and in newspapers because it was an important discovery.

But when other scientists tried to repeat their experiment, no one could make it work. The scientists had not discovered cold fusion after all. There were mistakes in the way they did their experiments.

Martin Fleischmann (left) and Stanley Pons (right) thought they had discovered cold fusion. Unfortunately they had made mistakes.

Correcting mistakes

After more tests by other scientists, a hypothesis can be proven correct and accepted. A very important part of the scientific method in the real world is putting an experiment out there for others to try. Science experiments have to be written down carefully to explain how they were done. Their results have to also be written down clearly so other scientists can understand them.

Many times in the past, people have come to wrong conclusions because their experiments had something wrong in them. That is why other scientists need to get the information and try it themselves. In science you do not have to take someone's word for something. You can test it out for yourself. That is one of the things that make the scientific method work in the real world. Many wrong conclusions have been corrected this way.

DID YOU KNOW?

Around 400 to 500 years ago, people used to blame witches when things went wrong. People believed that putting a woman into a lake would show whether or not she was a witch. If she floated, officials said it was proof that she was a witch. If she sank, she was not a witch. Were they using the scientific method?

Science Projects and Science Fairs

When you use the scientific method you should make sure you record everything carefully. Write up your experiment so that others can read what you did and do the same thing. Make sure your results are written in an easy-to-understand form.

Many students enter experiments in school science fairs. Often they do an excellent job of following the steps in the scientific method. But sometimes they only follow the steps correctly until they come to the conclusion.

Only conclude what you have proven

Drawing conclusions correctly is a very important part of the scientific method. A conclusion is a statement based on your results. It is important to make certain that the conclusion you draw is supported by evidence. If you follow the scientific method you will only conclude what is proven by your experiment. You must make sure you do not come to any conclusions that are not proven by your results.

A science lab notebook often shows experiment results in clearly labeled graphs and tables.

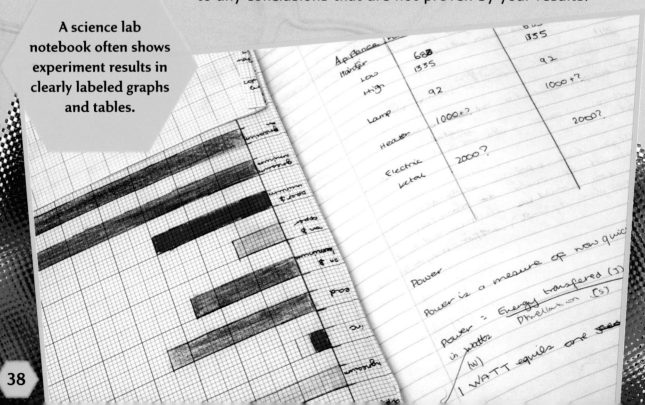

For example, say you did the dog food experiment from pages 10–13 of this book. All you proved was that your dog preferred one brand of food to another. If you said that he liked it because it was crunchier, that would be a false conclusion. You have not proven it. If you said most dogs like that brand better, that would be wrong. You have not proven that.

Going further

A conclusion includes information about any mistakes made during an experiment. Real scientists do this too. You could also discuss ways you might improve the experiment. You could mention further testing that would be useful. You could also suggest more research.

TOP TIP

Photographs of your experiment are an excellent way of showing your experiment on a science project display. Science fair organizers are always concerned about the safety of young children who might touch displays. So never have anything dangerous to children on your project display.

Careers Using the Scientific Method

The scientific method is something you can use in school. You can also use it if you work in a scientific job. Scientific study has been broken up into different branches. Earth science is the study of Earth, its oceans, its rocks, volcanoes and earthquakes, and its air and weather. Astronomy, the study of space, is usually included in Earth science.

Life science is the study of living things, including plants, animals, fungi, and microbes. The study of the human body is also part of life science.

Physical science is the study of matter and energy. Things such as light, heat, magnets, and electricity are part of this branch of science. Chemistry is included in physical science. Chemists study what things are made of and how they can change.

This scientist is studying a volcano. Protective clothing allows him to get close to the steam and lava.

Robots conduct experiments on Mars for scientists on Earth. The robots have found evidence that water once flowed on the surface of Mars. No evidence of life on Mars has turned up yet, even though the scientific method is being used to look for it!

The robot vehicle *Sojourner* took rock samples from Mars. Scientists could then learn more about the planet.

The scientific method at work

All the branches of science use the scientific method. Some scientists do investigations using computer models. For example, weather scientists use computer models to understand weather patterns and make predictions. They can predict hurricanes and other storms by feeding information into computers.

The scientific method is used in astronomy. Astronauts do investigations on the International Space Station. Robot spacecraft called space probes have explored and experimented on other planets.

Several years ago astronomers made a hypothesis that there must be another planet beyond Neptune. They even predicted where it would be. When astronomers searched that part of the sky, they discovered Pluto. Now they are finding more objects in the Solar System beyond Pluto. The steps of the scientific method get used every day in all branches of science.

Science on the job

You could work in the field of science when you grow up. There are still many questions to be answered and many problems to be solved. Or you could work in a job that requires a lot of science education, like medicine or engineering. Maybe you could be a science teacher.

Science has a huge impact on everyone's lives even if they do not work in a science related job. Remember, the scientific method is a way of solving problems and unraveling mysteries. The police use it to solve crimes. Public health agencies use it to stop disease and keep us healthy. If someone gets sick from eating food in a restaurant, investigators find out how it happened so it will not happen again.

This police investigator is carefully observing crime evidence and taking a photo-record.

Government employees study traffic patterns using computer models to figure out ways to prevent traffic jams. Automobile companies do experiments with crash test dummies on new models. They crash cars to find the safest designs. Every day plant scientists work to make better crops to feed the world.

Many companies have research and development departments of people using the scientific method to improve their products and create new ones. Lots of people use the scientific method every day on the job.

Crash test dummies are used to find out how car passengers could be protected in an automobile accident.

Think like a scientist

You can also use science in your daily life. Think like a scientist. Ask questions and find out all you can. You can research things on the Internet and in books. Ask people who might know about the subject, then make a hypothesis. Test it. Make sure you experiment carefully. Form a conclusion based on your results, making sure you only conclude what you have proven. You can find the answer to so many questions, big and small, in your life. The scientific method is a wonderful tool for learning about your world. Use it!

TRY IT!

As you go through your day, think of ways you can use the scientific method—at home, at school, anywhere. Look for ways other people use it without realizing.

Scientific Method Flowchart

OBSERVE AND ASK QUESTIONS

OBSERVE carefully. Do research. Think of a QUESTION you could answer by experimenting.

FORM A HYPOTHESIS

The HYPOTHESIS is what you think is the answer. It should be based on information. It is a statement that you can test.

PLAN AN EXPERIMENT

The EXPERIMENT is the way you test a hypothesis. The variables, all the things that could affect how it turns out, should be kept the same except for the one thing you are testing. Measurements should be made and recorded. Counting things is a way of measuring. Test things more than once.

CONDUCT THE EXPERIMENT

Follow your plan. Carefully observe and keep good records of your experiment. The results should be recorded in a way that makes it easy for others to understand.

DRAW CONCLUSIONS AND COMMUNICATE RESULTS

The CONCLUSION is where you decide if your RESULTS support your hypothesis or disprove it. Your experiment was successful either way. You learned something. Charts and graphs are good ways to communicate your results to others. If you kept good records, others can replicate, or copy, your experiment.

How to Record Information

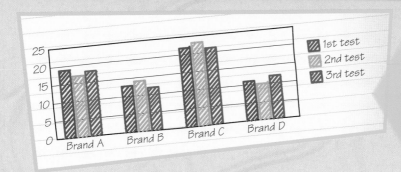

Bar charts are useful for comparing measurements or amounts in your results.

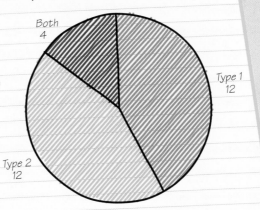

Results:
Preferred type 1: ‖‖‖‖‖‖‖‖‖ ‖‖
Preferred type 2: ‖‖‖‖‖‖‖‖ ‖‖
Liked both equally: ‖ ‖ ‖ ‖

Both
4

Type 1
12

Type 2
12

Pie charts clearly show fractions and percentages in study results.

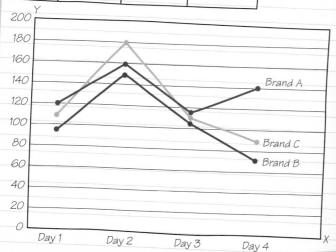

	Brand A	Brand B	Brand C
Day 1	120	95	110
Day 2	160	150	180
Day 3	115	105	110
Day 4	140	70	90

A line graph is a good choice if you are trying to show how something changes over time.

45

Glossary

absorb soak up a liquid

anthrax disease in animals that is caused by bacteria and can be passed to humans

bacteria one-celled living things that can only be seen through a microscope

cancer harmful disease in which some cells in the body grow wild and harmful

centimeter square square that is one centimeter wide and one centimeter long

cold fusion way to produce energy by joining the centers of atoms together without high temperatures; scientists have tried to achieve cold fusion without success

conclusion deciding after looking at the results of an experiment whether the hypothesis was correct or not

consumer group organization that works to guide and protect buyers of goods

control in an experiment, the control has the thing you are testing left out

experiment careful test to see if a hypothesis is correct

fungus (more than one are called fungi) living thing such as mold or a mushroom that may seem like a plant, but cannot make its own food like a plant

galaxy very large group of stars

graduated cylinder tube-shaped container marked with lines for measuring liquids or solids

graph diagram that shows the relationship between numbers

hypothesis answer to a question that can be tested by doing an experiment

identical exactly alike

invertebrate animal without a backbone

investigation using the scientific method to learn something

measurement finding the size or amount of something by comparing it to something else

microbe living thing too small to be seen without a microscope

model a representation of the real thing

observation learning with your senses, especially by seeing

placebo harmless pill containing no medicine

predict say what you think will happen

Renaissance great rebirth of learning in Europe that took place from the 1300s to 1500s

results how an experiment turns out, often using measurements

sample limited group that is tested in an investigation to learn something about a larger group

scientific method scientific way of finding things out, usually following these steps: observation, asking questions, forming a hypothesis, planning and conducting experiments, drawing conclusions, and sharing results

spore tiny, seed-like cell that can grow into a new fungus

subjective having to do with your feelings or opinions instead of the facts

vaccine shot or something swallowed that contains dead or weakened germs to protect against a disease

variable something that can be changed in an experiment

Further Reading

Cobb, Allan B. *Super Science Projects About Oceans*. New York: Rosen Publishing, 2005

Oxlade, Chris. *The Mystery of Life on Other Planets*. Chicago: Heinemann Library, 2002

Stewart, Gail B. *The Renaissance*. Farmington Hills, MI: Thomson Gale, 2005

Tracy, Kathleen. *Robert Koch and the Study of Anthrax*. Hockessin, DE: Mitchell Lane Publishers, 2004

Index